OCEANS ALIVE

Stingrays

by Martha E.H. Rustad

BELLWETHER MEDIA · MINNEAPOLIS, MN

Note to Librarians, Teachers, and Parents:

Blastoff! Readers are carefully developed by literacy experts and combine standards-based content with developmentally appropriate text.

Level 1 provides the most support through repetition of high-frequency words, light text, predictable sentence patterns, and strong visual support.

Level 2 offers early readers a bit more challenge through varied simple sentences, increased text load, and less repetition of high-frequency words.

Level 3 advances early-fluent readers toward fluency through increased text and concept load, less reliance on visuals, longer sentences, and more literary language.

Whichever book is right for your reader, Blastoff! Readers are the perfect books to build confidence and encourage a love of reading that will last a lifetime!

This edition first published in 2007 by Bellwether Media.

No part of this publication may be reproduced in whole or in part without written permission of the publisher. For information regarding permission, write to Bellwether Media Inc., Attention: Permissions Department, Post Office Box 1C, Minnetonka, MN 55345-9998.

Library of Congress Cataloging-in-Publication Data
Rustad, Martha E. H. (Martha Elizabeth Hillman),
  Stingrays / by Martha E.H. Rustad.
    p. cm. — (Oceans alive)
Summary: "Simple text and supportive full-color photographs introduce beginning readers to stingrays. Intended for kindergarten through third grade students"—Provided by publisher.
  Includes bibliographical references and index.
  ISBN-13: 978-1-60014-080-8 (hardcover : alk. paper)
  ISBN-10: 1-60014-080-7 (hardcover : alk. paper)
  1. Stingrays—Juvenile literature. I. Title.

QL638.8.R88 2007
597.3'5—dc22
                                                          2006035212

Contents

A stingray is a flat fish. Its wide **fins** look like wings.

Most stingrays live in the ocean. Some live in rivers or lakes.

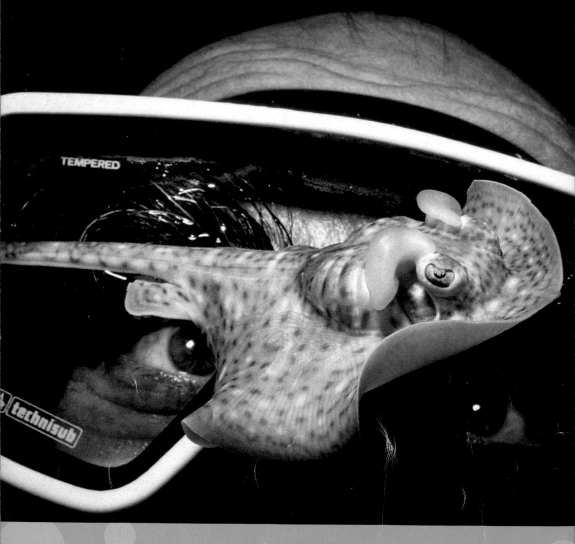

Some kinds of stingrays are as small as your hand.

Some kinds of stingrays are big. They can grow longer and wider than a car.

Most stingrays stay close
to the ocean floor.

They **blend** with the ocean floor. They hide from sharks that might try to eat them.

Some kinds of stingrays swim
near the top of the ocean.

They glide smoothly through the water. They can eat fish as they swim.

mouth

A stingray has a mouth on the bottom of its body.

A stingray eats fish, worms, shrimp, and clams.

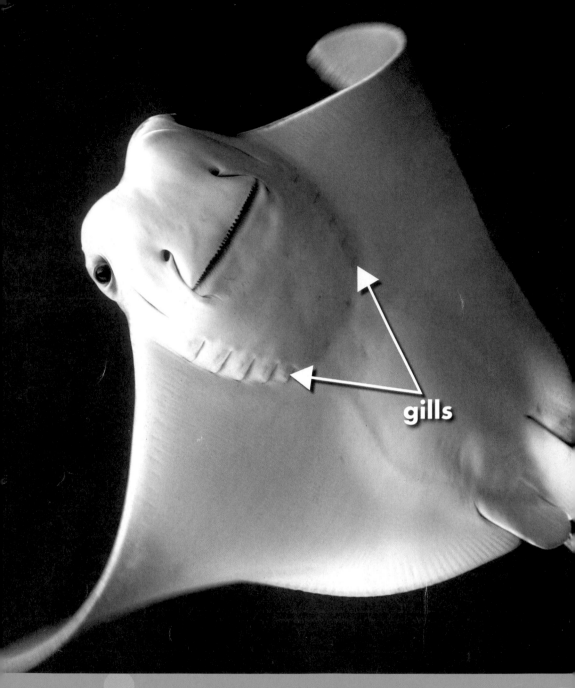

gills

A stingray has **gills** on the
bottom of its body. It uses
its gills to breathe.

14

A stingray has eyes on the top of its body.

A stingray has a long tail.

spine

A stingray has a **spine** on its tail.

The spine of a stingray has
many sharp points and
holds **poison**.

A stingray may sting people or fish if they come too close to it.

Most of the time a stingray
does not sting people or fish.

It swims quietly away
from them.

Glossary

blend—when something looks so much like the things around it that it becomes difficult to see

fins—thin parts that stick out from a fish's body; a fish uses fins to move through the water.

gills—slits near the mouth that a fish uses to breathe; the gills bring oxygen from the water to the stingray's blood.

poison—a substance that can hurt or kill another living thing

spine—a sharp body part that grows at the end or in the middle of the stingray's tail; some stingrays have two spines.

To Learn More

AT THE LIBRARY
Gross, Miriam J. *The Stingray: Weird Sea Creatures*.
New York: PowerKids Press, 2006.

Rake, Jody Sullivan. *Rays*. Mankato, Minn.: Capstone
Press, 2007.

Sharth, Sharon. *Sharks and Rays: Underwater
Predators*. New York: Franklin Watts, 2002.

Sjonger, Rebecca, and Bobbie Kalman. *Skates and
Rays*. New York: Crabtree, 2006.

ON THE WEB
Learning more about stingrays
is as easy as 1, 2, 3.

1. Go to www.factsurfer.com

2. Enter "stingrays" into search box.

3. Click the "Surf" button and you will see a list of
   related web sites.

With factsurfer.com, finding more information is just
a click away.

Index

The photographs in this book are reproduced through the courtesy of: Brad Thompson, front cover, p. 14; David Kearnes/Acclaim Images, p. 4; Macduff Everton/Getty Images, p. 5; Jeff Rotman/Alamy, pp. 6, 15; David Fleetham/Alamy, pp. 7, 10; Carlos Villoch/imagequestmarine, p. 8; Alain Machet/Alamy, p. 9; blickwinkel/Alamy pp. 11, 18(inset); Ian Scott, pp. 12-13, 20-21; Asther Lau Choon Siew, p. 16; Bill Curtsinger/Getty Images, p. 17; P. Robin Moeller, p. 18; Juan Martinez, p. 19.